Old BARNSLEY

by

CHRIS & PEARL SHARP

Originally named London Road, Sheffield Road was once a thriving shopping centre with all sorts of shops from a Post Office to a pawnbrokers. The tram route was from Worsbrough Dale and Worsbrough Bridge to Old Mill.

© 1993 Chris & Pearl Sharp
First Published in the United Kingdom, 1993
By Richard Stenlake, Ochiltree Sawmill, The Lade, Ochiltree, Ayrshire KA18 2NX
Tel: 02907 266

ISBN 1-872074-31-6

Sheffield Road and Tram Sheds, Barnsley. No. 2426.

Trams started operating in Barnsley in November 1902 and this view shows the depot on Sheffield Road. Traffic was brisk for the first few years but, by the end of World War One, business was tailing off. Buses had been encroaching on trade since before the war but an influx of ex-War Department vehicles and a new breed of entrepreneurs saw the setting up of many small one man bus companies. These competed with the trams by operating in areas the trams could not get to and by providing a faster service. Passenger numbers declined so much that the tramways finally ceased operating in August 1931. The depot is now used by Yorkshire Traction as a bus depot.

FOREWORD
by
Don Walton

Over the years developments in buildings, shops, street furniture and vehicles have changed the appearance of most towns and cities in our country. In Barnsley, this has been most noticeable in the town centre which has been re-developed since the end of World War Two. In many cases the picture postcard is the only visual record of everyday life in the first few decades of this century. The canvas covered stalls of Barnsley's open air markets drew vast crowds from all over the north of England. They have now been replaced by the indoor market and their sites built over and used as local government offices, car parks and pedestrianised areas. Like most towns, the cinemas have all but disappeared. From eight cinemas at their peak, Barnsley can now boast of only one. Names such as the Alhambra, the Ritz and the Pavilion are a distant memory to most. The ornate Victorian cast iron lamp standards have gone, as have most of the pillar boxes around the town. Trams and horses and carts have been replaced by motor cars and buses of all colours, and those local shops that still remain stock vastly different products from those visible in the following pictures.

This change is, of course, progress, but we hope that the reader will appreciate that it is sometimes good to look back and compare what we have now with what has been lost forever. For those old enough to remember some of these views, we hope they bring back happy memories.

In Barnsley, there were many very good photographers working at the turn of the century producing a unique record of this bygone era. Firms such as Lamb, Lodge, Denton, Warner Gothard, Irving and Haigh Bros are responsible for the pictures in the following pages, they have helped record life and scenes in the town for posterity.

MOUNT VERNON ROAD, BARNSLEY

Mount Vernon was once the stage coach route into the town from Sheffield and London. Since the excavation of the cutting at Worsburgh Dale it has become a quiet residential area.

3

The two ladies in their Sunday best have probably been out for a stroll to Locke Park. Park Road was renamed after Locke Park was opened. Originally it was called Johnny Warrener Lane.

THE "LANCASTER" CONVALESCENT HOME, BARNSLEY.

St. Edwards Vicarage Kingstone was used as a convalescent home for wounded soldiers during the First World War. The home was named after the benefactor of St. Edwards Church, George E. Lancaster.

Ebenezer Church, Barnsley.

The Ebenezer Church was at the junction of Sheffield Road and Doncaster Road. It was demolished in the name of road improvements and its site is now under the Alhambra Roundabout. The fountain behind the group of boys on the left provided drinking water for both horses and drivers.

6

This view shows the Alhambra just before it opened in 1915 as a 2500 seater theatre. It became a picture house in June 1925. Before being demolished its last use was as a bingo hall. Many happy Saturday mornings were spent queueing to see such matinees as Laurel and Hardy, The Krazy Gang, The Marx Bros. and Roy Rogers. A real treat was getting up into the gallery and watching the big screen from the back.

DONCASTER ROAD
BARNSLEY.

The main road into town from Doncaster was lit at night by the flickering glow of these cast iron lamps. Electricity was first used for street lighting in October 1900 and in 1954 the town started losing these beautiful ornate works of art as the first of many thousands of concrete lamp standards began to appear. St. Peter's Church on the left was consecrated in 1893 and restored in 1977. On the right is Doncaster Road School.

Visible in this view of New Street is J. Lodge's Stationers shop. He printed many of the views of the town in that golden age before World War One. In 1827, the first coals were pulled by horses from Porter's Pit down a tramroad along New Street and in 1893 there were a series of improvements and demolitions along here.

Cheapside, Barnsley.

Facing one of Barnsley's renowned open air markets, Cheapside was a major shopping area. In 1934, Bailey's had an illuminated stork erected on the roof of their shop which proclaimed "We supply all but the baby". Bailey's were established in 1880 and moved from Cheapside in 1968 to a new location in New Street.

Cheapside, Barnsley.

THORPE'S DRESS & DRAPERY WAREHOUSE

Wᴹ THORPE

Many people will still remember the junction of New Street, Cheapside, Sheffield Road and Pontefract Road where P.C. Bill Harber (the policeman with the handlebar moustache) controlled the traffic. The West Riding County Constabulary patrolled Barnsley's streets from January 1857 but Barnsley Borough Police took over in October 1896. It was in 25 Cheapside (on the left) that Albert Hirst, Pork Butchers was established in 1897. This firm originated the Barnsley Chop, now famous the world over, and in 1970 and 1971 they won two awards for their black puddings. The chain driven bus dates this view to before the First World War. Its solid rubber tyres would have given it a maximum speed of about 25 mph and a very uncomfortable ride over the cobbles in Cheapside.

This 1908 view of Mayday Green shows three different parts of the Barnsley Market and a tram running through the middle of it all. Behind the tram some tramway workers are repairing or checking the overhead tram wires.

The clock tower and bell were used to denote the closing time of the market.

SHOPPING WEEK. BARNSLEY.

Barnsley gained its charter to hold regular markets in 1249 and has held markets ever since. The market was first lit by electricity just in time for Christmas in 1909. Shopping Week was a grand occasion when the stall holders would decorate the market with bunting and flags. Sadly, now, Barnsley's famous markets have been lost to the new shopping centres and to the indoor market.

661 ELDON S^T, BARNSLEY.

This view, dating from 1904, shows the Harvey Institute which later became the Public Hall and is now the Civic Hall. Charles Harvey, who died in 1898, donated the Harvey Institute to the town. His estate was worth nearly £220,000 when he died.

Behind the horse trough and lamp standard is Denton's photographers.

In 1921, David Lloyd George, the Prime Minister, visited Barnsley when he was made a Freeman of the Borough. He's the small one in the top hat wearing the carnation. The Singer Sewing Machine shop is still in the same spot today.

Regent Street, Barnsley. No. 2882.

Left: Meetings of the Congregationalists commenced in 1836 and in November 1843 the foundation stone of the church in Regent Street was laid. But it was another thirteen years before the church opened for worship. In September 1971 the church closed when the congregation merged with Farrar Street to become the Trinity Church. Just below the church was the Courthouse Station.

Right: A proud regiment of Yorkshire Volunteers parades down Market Hill in 1904. Ten years later most of these men were called up to fight for their country in the war to end all wars. Many did not come back.

VOLUNTEER PARADE AT BARNSLEY. 25-6-04

The Obelisk & Huddersfield Road, Barnsley.

The Obelisk stood at the top of Old Mill Lane and was demolished in September 1931 after having been reprieved many times before that. It was first threatened by demolition in 1876 but was spared by the Council in 1886 and survived for almost another fifty years. In 1915, the year of this picture, neither the Obelisk nor the two gossiping ladies seem to have proved much of a hazard to traffic.

A relatively unchanged Huddersfield Road circa 1922 with one of the few motor cars then in the town coming up the street. It wasn't until the early 1930s that motoring became affordable and cars such as the original Morris Minor and Austin Seven could be bought for a hundred pounds or less.

18

Long after the Obelisk was removed, the clock (on the right) continued to give the time, even though the buildings in the background had been demolished. In 1965 the sign from the Old Mill Toll Bar was discovered and taken to Cannon Hall. Tolls were abolished on the Huddersfield and Penistone Turnpike Road in June 1876. At the present time, it looks like they will be re-introduced on some of our motorways, including the M1.

The horse drawn ice cream cart would have been licenced but it is unlikely that it would pass our more stringent health regulations nowadays. The ice cream was kept in tubs and sold before it melted. This scene, looking down Market Hill, shows a bustling part of the market. W.H. Smith's closed their store in Market Hill in 1973 and were the first retailer to move into the new Cheapside market complex.

This imposing building at the bottom of Market Hill has changed very little since 1913 when this view was taken. Previous to its use as a bank, the building was a hotel. The policeman seems to be having an easy life on points duty.

Shambles Street at this time projected out into Church Street. The shops have now been demolished. Although a few stalls are erected, it is evident that it is not market day.

Market Hill about 1910

This view shows Benjamin Harral's Ring Shop. Everyone who bought a wedding ring here received a wedding present free. Harral's sold all sorts of jewellery, spectacles and watches as well as leather goods and other small gifts. On the opposite side of Eldon Street one of the bus stands that were used before the bus station was built can be seen.

In the background can be seen the Market Inn and the canvas covered stalls of the May Day Green Market. At this time Queen Street was cobbled and very narrow. Today it is part of the pedestrian precinct.

Queen Street, Barnsley.

Queen Street looking towards Peel Square. In the foreground is the shop of Benjamin Gaunt. This well respected jeweller and watchmaker died in 1888. Next door but one is the Maypole Dairy. They were a national chain with branches in most British towns and have now totally disappeared from our high streets.

The first cabs for hire in Barnsley appeared in May 1865. A shelter was inaugurated in Peel Square in March 1888. This view has a mixture of horse drawn cabs and the first of the motor taxis that appeared in the town. For many people their first trip in a motor car would have been in one of these motor taxis which started running in the town as early as September 1908.

The foundation stone of Pitt Street Wesleyan Chapel (mid left) was laid in September 1845 and the Chapel opened soon after. It closed in the early 1900s for renovation and re-opened in July 1906. Many properties in Pitt Street (named after William Pitt, a former Prime Minister) have been demolished, including the Chapel and some of the last surviving weavers' cottages left in the town which were further up the hill.

Most of the buildings in Townend have gone. In the distance, along Racecommon Road, a solitary cow is walking up the middle of the road apparently unaccompanied. Photographers, though, were more of a novelty and just like TV today, everyone wanted to get in the picture. Given a choice between looking at the cow and posterity, most of the people have opted for the latter.

Bunting and flags fly as Townend is decorated for the Coronation of King George V on June 22nd, 1911. The celebrations included a proclamation, a day off school and street parties. Many of the children were given souvenirs of the event which still turn up at antique fairs today. Celebrations went on until the early hours of the 23rd in the Town Hall as the councillors celebrated and toasted the new King and the Empire.

York Street is one of the six streets that met at Townend. The building on the left is St. George's School which was closed in 1960. Beyond the school are the Public Baths. In June 1958, freak storms caused severe flooding at Townend. This area was under umpteen feet of water as was the Ritz Cinema.

Barnsley Corporation Baths opened in June 1874 and were expanded in 1913. New baths were opened to replace them in July 1914. This view shows the old Baths about 1907. Changing cubicles were down either side of the pool and there was a balcony for spectators.

Left: Shambles Street was noted for the large numbers of inns that it contained. It was formerly known as Westgate and was the road out of Barnsley to Penistone and Manchester.

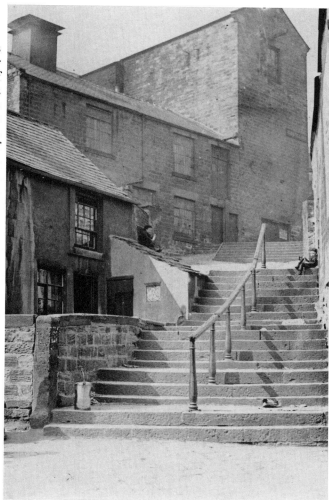

Right: Pinfold Steps about 1904.

The impressive Olympia Skating Rink was to be found at the junction of Peel Street and York Street. It opened in 1909. Workmen are still putting the finishing touches to the building in this view. After the novelty of rinking declined, the rink was converted into a cinema. The Pavilion Cinema, as it became, burned down in September 1950. The site is now occupied by the Pioneer Store and its car park.

The immaculately turned out staff of the Olympia Skating Rink sometime about 1910. The craze of rinking swept the country in 1908-9 and many purpose built rinks such as this were constructed. In an effort to draw the crowds, there were bands, waitresses at the tables and competitions to find the best roller skaters. You could even buy brand new skates in the shop.

Dodworth Road circa 1908. In the distance is a horse drawn removal van of a type once common in England and used by carriers such as Pickford's and Wordies.

One of the few wells serving the Barnsley area, Shaw Wells were patronised by many of the residents of the town. A horse drawn water cart would fill up here and tour the town selling water by the bucketful. Among the best customers were the weavers on the Sheffield Road area. A large quantity of water was used in linen manufacture, both to clean the cloth and to make it easier to weave.

Dodworth Road with the crowd of children unsure whether to look at the photographer or the more unusual motor car. This part of Dodworth Road has changed little in the eighty years since this picture was taken.

The Co-operative warehouse, factory and butchery departments can be seen in the background on the left. The cooked meat factory closed in January 1972, making 33 people redundant. Dodworth Road is almost deserted in this view from circa 1914, unlike today when it is the main road to the M1.

EMPIRE DAY, MAY 24TH 1911.
RACECOMMON ROAD SCHOOLS BARNSLEY.

Everybody out in their Sunday best for Empire Day. Celebrated on May 24th, Empire Day has since become Commonwealth Day and largely forgotten about. In 1911, Britain was truly a world power and Empire Day was an important event. Children spent the day celebrating a day off school-work and there were parades and displays.

A view of Park Grove originally published on a postcard by Lamb. The children are eager to have their photograph taken in this quiet residential street.

DRINKING FOUNTAIN LOCKE PARK BARNSLEY

Joseph Locke was born in 1805 and became one of Victorian England's most eminent railway engineers. He designed and supervised the construction of the Grand Junction Railway from Birmingham to Warrington. This line, opened in 1837, was the first British trunk railway. It later became part of the London & North Western Railway along with the Lancaster & Carlisle Railway, another of Locke's designs. Locke also designed and supervised construction of the Caledonian Railway's main line to Glasgow from Carlisle. He was ultimately responsible for over half of the West Coast Main Line. He died in 1860.

The park was presented to the town by Locke's widow, Phoebe, and opened in June 1862. A statue to the great man was erected in 1866. The drinking fountain in the previous picture originally resided in Peel Square but was moved to the park in 1866. It originally had a cup on a chain which has been missing for a long time and the fountain was, at one time, used as a flower pot!

The columns which give this path its name of Corinthian Walk were moved in 1871. They were originally part of the facade of the Post Office building in Church Street and were known locally as Matthew, Mark, Luke and John. The message on the back of this 1906 postcard tells the recipient that this was "Not a bad area for spooning on a summer night."

LOCKE PARK, BARNSLEY.

The tower was designed by a Mr. Spiers and was opened in August 1877 by Viscount Halifax. Subsidence caused by mining led to the tower being closed in 1966. It was repaired in 1973-4. Other additions to the park were the bandstand in 1908, a tea pavilion in 1911 and a bowling green in 1922.

King George V and Queen Mary visited Barnsley in July 1912. One of the places they visited was Messrs. Rylands Glass & Engineering Works where they saw a six foot high glass arch made to commemorate their visit.

BARNSLEY'S TANK,
JULY 1st, 1919.

The tank, pictured here in Peel Square, was given to the town at the end of the war. Its armament, removed before the tank was given to the town, would have included two cannons and several machine guns. The tank was moved to Locke Park and eventually broken up for scrap. Tanks were introduced during World War One and first saw action in France and Belgium where they terrified the Germans on their first outings. Many towns were given a tank after the end of the war but many were lost in the scrap metal drives of World War Two.

46

Left: Battling Barnsley eventually beat West Brom in extra time after an action-packed replay at Bramall Lane, Sheffield on April 24th, 1912. Jimmy Moore, the last surviving member of the Cup-winning team, died in December 1972, the same year that Barnsley were relegated to the Fourth Division.

Right: "Amos", Barnsley Football Club's mascot is pictured on his donkey outside the Clarence Hotel. This was the headquarters of the Club at one time, Amos obviously brought luck to the team in 1912.

LAW-ABIDING

F.P 594. Pilgrim Suffragettes, Barnsley, July 4. 1913.

These formidable looking ladies were the Pilgrim Suffragettes who travelled the country in an attempt to change our political system and give women the vote. While some suffragettes believed in violent action (Emily Davidson from Northumberland who threw herself in front of the King's horse at the Derby being just one example of militant suffragettes) the Pilgrim Suffragettes believed in peaceful action. They wore the uniform of green, white and purple rosettes and ribbons. It was not until after World War One that women were granted the right to vote.

MINERS DEMONSTRATION. BARNSLEY. JUNE 20TH 1904 Barnsley Photo Co.

Every four or five years the Miners' Demonstration would come to Barnsley. The miners paraded with brass bands and large banners before being addressed by their leaders. In 1904, they marched from Peel Square in seven sections to Mark Oldham's Field, off Racecommon Road. They started at noon heading along Shambles Street, Market Hill, Peel Street and then along Racecommon Road. The speeches were at 1.30 p.m. and one of the main speakers was Keir Hardie, the Scottish Independent Labour M.P.

After the end of World War One, the Barnsley Pals returned to the town. Here, they are assembled on Market Hill, being addressed by Lt. Colonel Sir Joseph Hewitt, after marching from a special parade at Queen's Ground. The occasion was to say farewell to the Colours.

RETURN OF THE BARNSLEY
BATTALIONS, MAY 29th, 1919.
COLOURS ENTERING S. MARY'S CHURCH.

The colours arrived at St. Mary's Church where a service was held.

The Fruit Market a hive of activity sometime in 1905. In the background is the railway line to Courthouse Station. The station was opened in May 1870. It closed to traffic in April 1960 and Barnsley Exchange was renamed Barnsley Station then. In September 1962, the Courthouse Station saw a new lease of life as a dancehall. Barnsley Corporation bought the building in 1967 for over £60,000.

REGENT STREET, BARNSLEY.

This view shows the Regent Street entrance of the Midland and Great Central Railway station. The branch to Barnsley, from Dodworth, was nearly three miles long and opened early in 1857. There were four or five major bridges on the line, the most notable being at Old Mill Lane the line split with one railway joining with the Lancashire and Yorkshire Railway line and the other entering a large goods yard capable of taking over 400 waggons at any one time.

The Arcade decorated for the Coronation celebrations in 1911. It was protected from the elements by a glass roof and held a treasure trove of dealers in all sorts of goods including clothes, furniture, stationery and, most important of all, toys. Kids would stand with their noses pressed to the windows at Ogley's admiring the tinplate railway engines and china dolls that filled the shelves.

Some of the staff of the Beckett Hospital pose outside in the garden circa 1910.

LANDING WHERE ACCIDENT OCCURRED.

PUBLIC HALL BUILDING.

CROWD OUTSIDE HALL

1. BEATRICE CARTWRIGHT.
2. ALICE MARSHALL.
3. HENRY WILLIAMS.
4. JOHN CHARLES HIBBERT.
5. FLOSSIE SMITH.
6. MARY LEE.
7. ALBERT WARD.
8. JOHN CHARLES GRAHAM.
9. HARDY STOTT.
10. MARY STOTT.
11. NELLIE SWIFT.
12. EDWARD PICKLES.
13. ANNIE JOHNSON.
14. WINNIE COUSINS.
15. CHARLOTTE NORTON.
16. WILLIAM PARKIN GOODALE.

BECKETT HOSPITAL.

WAGNER BERNARD, Photo. Barnsley.

PUBLIC HALL, BARNSLEY, SATURDAY, JANUARY 11th, 1908.

ENTRANCE TO GALLERY.

A SAD CALAMITY OCCURRED, IN WHICH 16 CHILDREN LOST THEIR LIVES.

On Saturday, January 11th, 1908 sixteen children lost their lives in what became known as the Barnsley Public Hall Disaster. The children were entering the Public Hall to see a matinee when someone inside the hall shouted out the fatal word "Fire!" In their rush to get out there was a stampede. Some of the children fleeing the supposed fire fell as they met others still climbing the narrow stairs to the gallery. Panic had set in and, in the ensuing crush, the sixteen children picture above, the oldest of whom was only nine, were crushed or asphyxiated to death. The survivors were taken to the Beckett Hospital. Tragically there had been no fire!